wolf mutter

a poem by

K. Blasco Solér

Finishing Line Press
Georgetown, Kentucky

wolf mutter

Publisher: Leah Huete de Maines

Editor: Christen Kincaid

Cover Art: K. and Paul Blasco Solér

Author Photo: Mary Alves de Campos

Cover Design: Elizabeth Maines McCleavy

Order online: www.finishinglinepress.com

also available on amazon.com

Author inquiries and mail orders:

Finishing Line Press

PO Box 1626

Georgetown, Kentucky 40324

USA

CONTENTS

for my mother
on every page

wolf mutter

in a den | dawn | finding solace in her image |
after tidal waves | mooncalf | subsumed by wild
ness | cairn of memory | desire | dragonfly | fallen
leaves | termination dust | the most inflexible still
gathering scars | bristlecone pine | researching
wolves | struggle through | bound in willow
| in various states of destruction and
resurgence | after give of tundra
beneath | always returning
to alpine lake

in a den
        of mud and stone
where woven roots
   bind our blood together

where light filters
   through the undergrowth

   you found a place
to sleep and breathe
     with your beloved

   your final retreat
from the cold the excommunicated
those who rid themselves of you

past and present
   marauding predators
 your own iterations

when I emerge
        after your death
    to track for enormous prints
studded with claws
I find raw blood
    in snow memory

wind in their black fur
        and gray and brown
    and white
blowing in all directions
a haunting
    around the eyes

I tried to draw a wolf
        as a little girl
    and did not yet understand
what it is
        to have a haunt
to be beholden to   yet still leave
            only to be left in turn
by wolf   by mother |

dawn so my want silence is not formed
black of irises silent conception one was
sewing outside my chest my thorax silk in
writing black iris formation black words
the folds not the conception outside lifted
off one's haunches to not want it to give
up we don't have the words ocean of black
irises living in darkness of where one sits |

finding solace in her image   a wolf emerging
from the regional extirpation of her kind
by wild dispersal   the length of her
pink stippled tongue hanging
in   anxious   alarm
the wide angle
of her ears and their warm
capillaries and cartilage wrapped
in a density of fine fur   a mask
over   dark   seeing   eyes
markings of a hunter
the hunting of her
and the length of her ribcage
rippling into a chasm connected
by her spine to the darker
pelvic   cage   keep
the bloodlining bearing all future children |

after tidal waves
   of rage and desire
  the blood feuds
installed and out of body
   I released myself
from implantation's window
  my daughter in the wings
or a sleight of hand
  I didn't want it   enough
but I did want it   enough
   that we were not   not living
    not   not dying

will this punishing loss
one day   be punishable still |

mooncalf

defined as a foolish or absentminded person
originally   a false pregnancy or growth
in the womb

what mooncalves have I made   products
of supposedly bad moons   my own
absentmindedness   or deformity

I was her mooncalf
        she shed the cradle
that carried me
she said I clung for dear life   to her insides
perhaps my mother lives there now   in mine

she clings to me
with the most delicate claws
        she clings |

subsumed by wildness
another womb we are within
tired of looking inward
    now treading gently out
    and along beloved Mount Blue Sky

the new yet old name given as redress
is partial at best   not enough to honor those subsumed by
historical and ongoing
violence   for land | power

my ancestral brand's   tender raised edge
is not a scar   but a sign
    still burning |

cairn of memory
    the Peoples' Crossing
where I become us
yet never again on such embattled ground will I hear
  where are you from?
    and believe it is an innocuous question
with its too often implied proximity to
        where do you belong?
the People's Crossing
    what a generous offering
to be so entrusted |

desire for trust moves these
blue green eyes back and forth

and other ecological kin appear
in place of human guardians

a mountainside where I wade into alpine willow
outcropping of rock pink sky blizzard a moose

old pine along the Flatirons Fountain Formation
a prairie dog town disturbing manicured grounds

sanctuary of wild raspberry taking over
a chain link border fence from my childhood

here is the bunker where I store things
to share later upon Eldorado Mountain

past the red gas masked Cold War Horse memorializing
the decommissioned Rocky Flats
the plutonium trigger manufacturing facility once
considered among Earth's most polluted sites

we climb the dog and I against strong air currents
streaming over the Front Range from the west as she
runs at top speed such exhilaration curiosity
despite aging hips and the limitations of captive life

I step over winter withered cacti crushed grass
turn to survey the plains to the east and Denver
its geometric cluster a stack of pyrite
our little bit of fool's gold

on the way up we pass the bunker not unlike the
one where I danced on a bluff outside Anchorage
with its own decommissioned cold war relics
all the things we are decommissioning inside us

I'm afraid of repeating history
the little wars that happen when you let
people in when you whittle down the ramparts

I keep everything at such a distance
as a preventative measure a shelter against
but grief radiates all the same

actively weaponized inside and out
like the radionuclides resting at the bottom
of the lake from which my community drinks

but this resilient landscape this only partially
domesticated animal of such underacknowledged
intelligence could not be more open |

dragonfly ailing on the sidewalk
running alongside the now open flow
of Farmer's Canal

your blue green body still iridescent upside down
Kafkaesque with legs akimbo

such transparent wings broad with all their veins
and margins intact but still as anything as nothing

take it home keep it with the desiccated cicada
of similar hue carried all the way from Texas to
Colorado in a small box made of bloodstone

                    but you're still alive
my knuckle brushes against your tiny
black appendages   still kicking
the orbs of your mirrored eyes' a silent reflection
a gentle tumble right side up on spindly legs

can one little death be postponed
if only for a moment

                    it begins to rain |

fallen leaves
gather in footfalls the unforgotten
    of my crusted snowdrift depressions dark water
ripples under the ice that breaks into long blades
along the most tender fault lines and it is
                        coaxed into the current
a reintegration with
    the moving body

    a floe breaks into smaller pieces and
I am only peripherally harmed by the fractured why
hold myself frozen when others when she
found it so hard   to stay alive

 give way
    to the breakup season
with its flow of winter's passing

into spring
 river's rapids |

termination dust
over summits
a full and diffuse moon

black ridge
an almost as dark sky
the inky silhouette
of a lone elk
stands still at the crest
the moment I am compelled to look
descending
into the impossible weight
of a mountain

a stand of aspen
in its most golden aspect
of temporary   not entire
resignation
that greater vigor
come spring

a stunning coyote
      almost mistaken for a wolf
in the golden hour
      sitting in a sunlit prairie
its coat silvery against swaying grasses
      the contrast
         catches

and a hawk in flight at Medicine Bow
      hovers in midair
      over the edge of a plateau
gripped by tundra

      converging winds
         ruffle the ends of wings
where they meet
      wind suspends
her prey
   a temporary captive
         carried across
even stillness
      isn't static |

the most inflexible still gathering scars grow softer
in the supple movement   of ongoing survival |

bristlecone pine
dwelling for as many as two millennia
on this massif the region's most northern stand
12,000 feet above the sea
imagine the centuries' doldrums and dramas
the gales 200 mph and such freezes and inhospitably
parched soil
but here southern facing branches twist in the sun free of
disease with the banishing magic
of tight growth rings a pine's twisting
is a wringing in drinking every drop given to bend
along the arcs of our confusion and conflict
and momentary peace
it plays out as gnarled branches conserve energy dropping
needles once a decade and how many
do I drop in a year like the average pine
bristlecone stripbarking can salvage and carry
the still living in this winding shrine
the world's highest rock garden |

researching wolves I learn the finer details of
howling barking growling whingeing for the hunt
celebration high alert *storm is coming strange
business* great distances between them as many
as 50 miles their howls harmonic 150-780 Hz
12 overtones she wolves sound a great *U* nasally
baritone modulated males sing within an octave *O*
with bass finish the young say *Oooooooo* and
UuuuUuuUu Yip yip scent marks the spot leg lift
squat precaudal scent glands on dorsal tail anal
gland secretions on scat vaginal tell tail apocrine
and eccrine sweat glands between the claws as
they anticipate threats food friends who lick
faces rub cheeks push noses jostle jaws with
posture of ears up and pinned neutral tail hanging
soft gaze submissive and sleek with tucked tail
tongue out while aggressors stand tall mouths
open tongue in raised tail quivers piloerection of
hackles around the neck and withers between the
shoulders thrill of goose bumps with a purpose |

struggle through Storm Pass
sink hip deep
watching blue sky
  notice a buck watching
 from a clearing across the hillside
continue along the packed trail
winding through tunnels of
gooseneck aspen
tufted fir
  our heartbeats quicken
as we trust fall to disappear
 into powder drifts just off trail
   to watch a winter squirrel
and mountain chickadee
 undisturbed in the exposed
   bearberry's red fruits
in the shadow of meringue
 topped boulders edged
  with pale green lichen
  felled trees
 where mushrooms thrive
an eagle soars over the ridge
 attentive to a wary start of elk

see what comes of the burn area
along the entire mountain face
charred stubble against snow
all so eerily open

look closer and see
what painstaking new growth
lichen along carbon trapping coal
soft pine sprouts where the sun hits

is anything here
ever really destroyed |

bound in willow
the incongruent parts burst
with gentle force field of broken
branches and mud for miles
a clipping glitch in the season
a red shafted feather flies
as coffers in the sky
rain indiscriminate bullets
from unknown sources
near the high school
as clustered flowers
ping off nearby park benches
we wait for the text message
that says it's ok to flee our bodies
still intact blood brimming

notice the finest fur on this
flower both male and female
witness them reaching over stones
under which the creeping thistle
sprouts spines and dreams
of drawing blood in months
in hours minutes moments
under a nest of northern flickers
their bright black spotted wings
bellies bursting with early worms |

in various states of destruction and resurgence
the wilderness is not out there but in here |

after give of tundra beneath and flush of wind
burn   after perilous snowfield   after listening
for the howl and just missing it   after the sound
of mountains gathering thunder and belaboring
trails and breathlessness   after mountain goats

and hailstorms   after prophetic pupils of wild
sheep   after pronghorns in various pastures
after the signaling of marmots in the talus and
the rut of elk in the valley   after the deadening
and the ice formation   after desert boulder
scrambling and desiccated mornings   after
perpetually burning coal seams and wildfires

after countless descents along the spine I have
let it all thin out like oxygen at the summit to
expand beyond perceivable limits becoming
larger   more attenuated   less tumultuous and
severe   leaving parts of myself behind   not in
abandon   but safe keeping |

always returning to alpine lake
　　　　highest
rock bottom
　　　interspecies communion
　　　　　below jagged ridgeline
　　　　　　SCREE
shoreline of soft tundra plateau
pressed in glacial silt
　　　　　splay
　　　　　　low barometric
　　　　gnarled pine
the only shrine
　　　　　an after | life
　　　in memoriam of all the loved lost ones
the ones before lost who could be loved
a homing for what is   after all
　　　　clusters of ice blue forget me nots
　　　　　moss campion
　　　　　kinnikinnik |

NOTES AND ACKNOWLEDGMENTS

Page 4 includes text from Leslie Scalapino's
New Time.

Page 5 references Bhanu Kapil's *Humanimal:
A Project for Future Children.*

Page 8 was prompted by an Instagram post by
Ariana Reines dated April 21, 2023:
*My stomach is where my grandmother lives.
It is also where my mother—yes, lives.*
https://www.instagram.com/p/CrTOc_CsNS9/?hl=en.
The definition and etymology of *mooncalf* is courtesy
of Merriam Webster.

Page 9 refers to the Colorado chapter of the KKK:
https://www.denverpost.com/2021/06/06/denver-
kkk-history/https://www.historycolorado.org/
kkkledgers. The beloved mountain referenced here was
officially renamed Mount Blue Sky in September 2023.

"People's Crossing" on page 10 references the
renaming of Settler's Park in Boulder, June 2021:
https://bouldercolorado.gov/projects/peoples-crossing.
The passage was prompted by Bo Hwang's moving
land acknowledgement speech as host of Naropa's
regional 5x5 MFA reading at the Harry Smith Print
Shop in Boulder, November 2022.

Page 12 references the history of Rocky Flats:
https://cumulis.epa.gov/supercpad/SiteProfiles/index.
cfm?fuseaction=second.cleanup&id=0800360
and Kincaid Bunker in Anchorage, Alaska.

Page 15 is dedicated to Boulder Creek and healing conversations along its waters with Kristina Benson.

Bristlecone pine stats on page 19 are courtesy of the Mt. Goliath division of Denver Botanic Gardens.

Most of the wolf howl details on page 20 come from *Of Wolves and Men* by naturalist Barry Lopez.

Page 22 is prompted by and dedicated to Natasha Pepperl and the 2022-2023 Lighthouse Poetry Collective mentored by Carolina Ebeid.

Pages 23-24 references incidents of gun violence in and around Denver and Boulder schools: https://everystat.org/#Colorado.

The passage on page 25 is inspired by the inter-species work of Donna Haraway and Anna Tsing. The term resurgence comes from the ecological justice scholarship of Kyle Whyte.

Page 26's form and anaphora is inspired by Sueyeun Juliette Lee's "The Black Magma Inside You" from *Aerial Concave Without Cloud*.

Page 27 is dedicated to wolf man Andrew Schelling. SCREE is from Gary Snyder's *Earth House Hold*. Kinnikinnik is the Indigenous Algonquian word for the arctic and alpine low-bush bearberry, Arctostaphylos.

IN GRATITUDE

Deepest thanks for the mentorship and editorial
eyes of Carolina Ebeid and Jeffrey Pethybridge; the
intrepid spirits of Anne Waldman, Valerie Hsiung, and the
Pillowbook Collective led by Michelle Naka Pierce; and
to Finishing Line Press' New Women's Voices Chapbook
Competition for the gift of being read. Love always to
my partner Paul Blasco Solér for his tireless support and
encouragement.

The writing of *wolf mutter* coincided with a two-year independent study of the extermination and reemergence of gray wolves in the Southern Rockies, including interviews with renowned wolf biologists (including "the Jane Goodall of wolves" Diane Boyd), consultations with Naropa's Professor Andrew Schelling, and remote retreats in Colorado wolf territory. The resulting sequence explores psychogeography, matrilineal connection, and intergenerational trauma. *wolf mutter* weaves through personal and collective grief, capacities for survival, and the communion of delicate ecologies.

K. Blasco Solér's larger work, *engulf*, includes *wolf mutter* and two other bioregional poem sequences influenced by many years living in and traveling through the Pacific Northwest and Texas. An early version of the collection was a finalist for the 2023 Colorado Prize for Poetry. K's poems have appeared in *tiny SPOON, Bombay Gin, Wild Roof Journal*, and *Dark Matter*. K holds an MFA in creative writing and poetics from the Jack Kerouac School at Naropa University in Boulder. Currently in Gainesville, K teaches writing and literature while completing a PhD in English at the University of Florida.

www.ingramcontent.com/pod-product-compliance
Lightning Source LLC
Chambersburg PA
CBHW022055080426
42734CB00009B/1353